What's So Good about Vegetables?

By Ronne Randall

Gareth Stevens Publishing
A WORLD ALMANAC EDUCATION GROUP COMPANY

Please visit our web site at: www.garethstevens.com
For a free color catalog describing Gareth Stevens Publishing's list of
high-quality books and multimedia programs, call 1-800-542-2595 (USA)
or 1-800-387-3178 (Canada). Gareth Stevens Publishing's fax: (414) 332-3567.

Library of Congress Cataloging-in-Publication Data

Randall, Ronne.
　　What's so good about vegetables? / by Ronne Randall.
　　　　p. cm. — (What? Where? Why?)
　　Includes index.
　　Summary: Discusses the nutritional value of various kinds of foods.
　　ISBN 0-8368-3789-4 (lib. bdg.)
　　　1. Nutrition—Juvenile literature. 2. Diet—Juvenile literature.
　　[1. Nutrition.] I. Title. II. Series.
　　QP141.R29　2003
　　613.2—dc21　　　　　　　　　　　　　　　　2003045743

This North American edition first published in 2004 by
Gareth Stevens Publishing
A World Almanac Education Group Company
330 West Olive Street, Suite 100
Milwaukee, Wisconsin 53212 USA

Original copyright © 2003 by ticktock Entertainment Ltd. First published in Great Britain in 2003
by ticktock Media Ltd., Unit 2, Orchard Business Centre, North Farm Road, Tunbridge Wells,
Kent, TN2 3XF, England. This U.S. edition copyright © 2004 by Gareth Stevens, Inc.

Gareth Stevens series editor: Dorothy L. Gibbs
Gareth Stevens cover design: Melissa Valuch

Picture Credits
[Abbreviations: (t) top, (b) bottom, (c) center, (l) left, (r) right]
Alamy Images: pages 4(bl), 11(tr), 13(tr), 16(bl).
Comstock: pages 14(bl), 24(bl).
Corbis: pages 1(all), 2(all), 3(all), 4(cl, t-all, bc, br), 5(all), 6(all), 7(all), 8(all), 9(all), 10(all), 11(bl, bc, br),
12(all), 13(tl, b-all), 14(tl, tc, tr, br), 15(all), 16(tl, cr), 17(tl, tc, tr), 18(all), 19(all), 20(all), 22(all), 23(all), 24(tr).
Creatas: front cover.

Every effort has been made to trace the copyright holders for the pictures used in this book.
We apologize in advance for any unintentional omissions and would be pleased to insert the
appropriate acknowledgements in any subsequent edition.

With thanks to: Lorna Cowan, Sarah Schenker at the British Nutrition Foundation, and Elizabeth Wiggans.

Printed in Hong Kong

1 2 3 4 5 6 7 8 9 07 06 05 04 03

CONTENTS

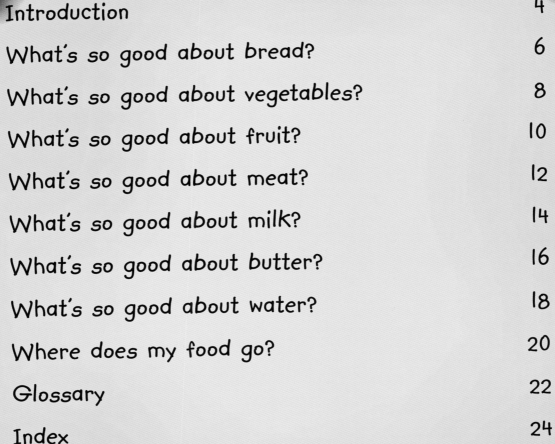

Words in the glossary are printed in **boldface** type the first time they appear in the text.

Food tastes good, and
it can be fun to eat.
But why is food
good for your body?

4

Food makes you feel better when you are hungry. But even more important, eating a **balanced diet**, which includes lots of different foods, gives your body the **nutrients** it needs to stay healthy and strong.

The foods in the meal shown below come from six important groups. Together, they provide a good mix of the nutrients that make up a balanced diet.

Have you ever wondered what's so good about these foods?

salad

milk

fruit

meatballs and tomato sauce

ice cream

bread and butter

spaghetti

What's so good about bread?

Bread is a **carbohydrate** food.

bread and butter

So is pasta, rice, or cereal. Crackers and potatoes are carbohydrate foods, too.

These foods give you long-lasting **energy**. They help you run and play without getting tired right away.

They also give you **fiber**, which is good for your **digestive system**.

Popcorn, sandwiches, and baked potatoes are some favorite carbohydrate treats.

Throughout this book, portions of this food pyramid symbol will show you how many servings from each food group you should eat each day.

What country does spaghetti come from?

(answer on page 23)

You need 6 to 10 **servings** of carbohydrates every day.

6–10

What's so good about vegetables?

Crunchy carrots, leafy spinach, crisp lettuce, and cool cucumbers are real superfoods.

salad

These vegetables all have important **vitamins** and **minerals** your body needs.

Carrots have vitamin A to help your eyes see better in the dark.

The B vitamins in spinach help your body turn food into energy.

Which vegetable is actually a fruit?
(answer on page 23)

8

Cucumbers have a mineral called potassium that helps your muscles work.

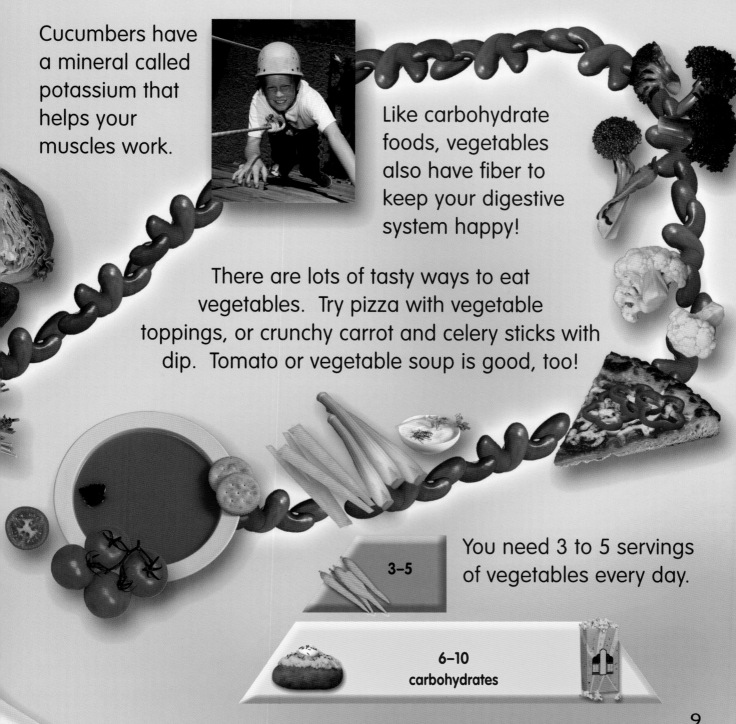

Like carbohydrate foods, vegetables also have fiber to keep your digestive system happy!

There are lots of tasty ways to eat vegetables. Try pizza with vegetable toppings, or crunchy carrot and celery sticks with dip. Tomato or vegetable soup is good, too!

3–5

You need 3 to 5 servings of vegetables every day.

6–10
carbohydrates

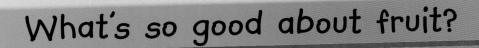

fruits

Juicy oranges, tangy pineapple, sweet strawberries — how many other delicious fruits can you think of?

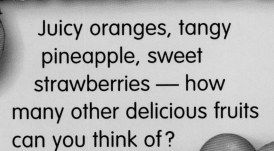

All fruits are packed with vitamins.

Oranges have lots of vitamin C.

Among other things, vitamin C keeps your gums healthy.

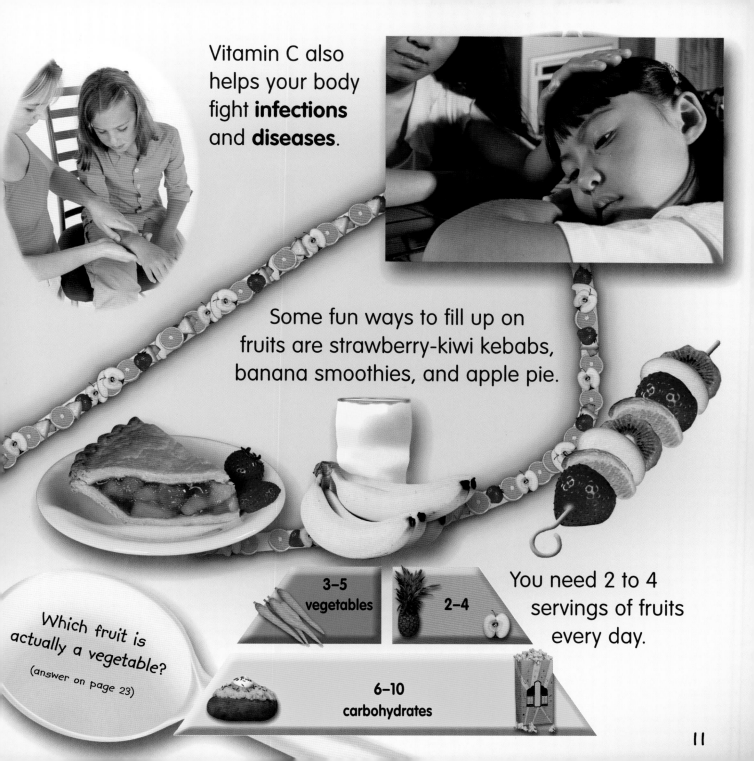

Vitamin C also helps your body fight **infections** and **diseases**.

Some fun ways to fill up on fruits are strawberry-kiwi kebabs, banana smoothies, and apple pie.

You need 2 to 4 servings of fruits every day.

Which fruit is actually a vegetable?

(answer on page 23)

3–5 vegetables

2–4

6–10 carbohydrates

What's so good about meat?

Meat, whether it's meatballs, turkey, lamb chops, or steak, has lots of **protein**.

Fish, eggs, and nuts have protein, too.

meatballs

Your body uses protein to make new muscle and skin **cells**.

Some people do not eat meat or fish. Do you know what these people are called? (answer on page 23)

12

All of these foods also have **iron**, which is an important mineral for healthy blood.

Some delicious ways to eat protein are poached eggs, hot dogs, fish sticks, and cheeseburgers.

You need 2 to 3 servings of protein foods every day.

2–3

3–5
vegetables

2–4
fruits

6–10
carbohydrates

What's so good about milk?

Dairy products, such as ice cream, cheese, and yogurt, are all made from milk.

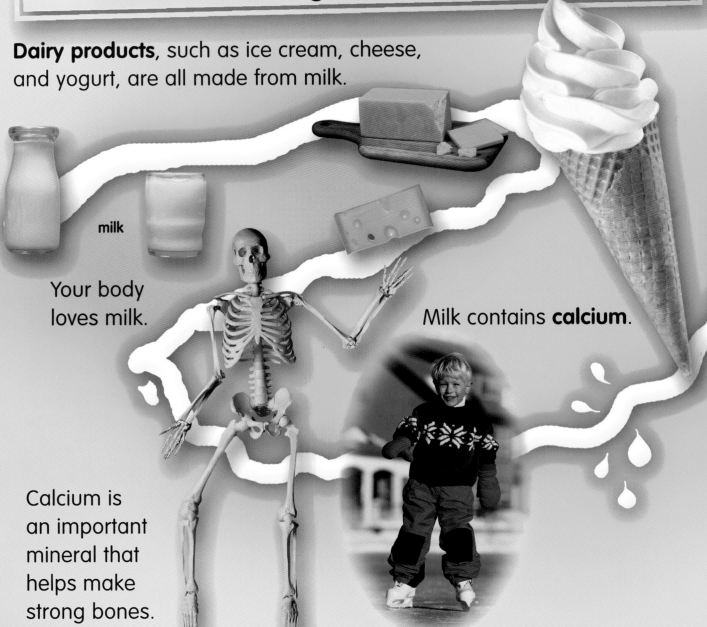

milk

Your body loves milk.

Milk contains **calcium**.

Calcium is an important mineral that helps make strong bones.

Calcium also keeps your teeth strong.

A cool way to get calcium is to eat yogurt with fruit.

Cheesy pizzas and milkshakes are good, too.

What animals do we get milk from?
(answer on page 23)

You need 2 to 3 servings of dairy products every day.

protein foods — 2–3

2–3

3–5 vegetables

2–4 fruits

6–10 carbohydrates

What's so good about butter?

Butter and margarine have lots of **fat**.

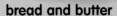

bread and butter

Your body needs some of the fat in butter, margarine, and vegetable oils.

Fat helps your body **absorb** some of the vitamins from the other foods you eat.

But too much fat is bad for you.

Which contains the most fat, a package of potato chips or a doughnut?

(answer on page 23)

Some foods have too much fat. Even worse, some of them also contain lots of sugar and salt.

Once in a while, it's all right to eat candy, cookies, and potato chips — as a treat!

But remember to leave room for all the good foods your body needs.

Eat only small amounts of fat and sugar each day.

protein foods — 2–3

dairy products 2–3

3–5 vegetables

2–4 fruits

6–10 carbohydrates

And remember to brush your teeth at least twice a day to keep them healthy!

17

What's so good about water?

Your body is made up of skin, hair, bones, muscles, blood — and lots of water!

If you weigh 40 pounds (18 kilograms), more than 26 pounds (12 kg) of that is water.

Every day, your body loses some of its water.

Exercise that makes you sweat, going to the toilet, and even just breathing all make you lose water.

Your body tells you when you have lost a lot of water by making you thirsty.

Even before you feel thirsty, you should drink water and other **fluids**, such as milk or fruit juice, to put back water you have lost.

You can also get fluids by eating fruits and vegetables that have a lot of water in them. Good ones to choose are tomatoes, grapes, cucumbers, and melons.

You should drink 6 to 8 glasses of fluids every day.

Which fruit or vegetable contains the most water?
(answer on page 23)

Where does my food go?

Now you know that food not only tastes good but is good for your body, too!

vitamins, minerals, and fiber

fat

carbohydrates and fiber

calcium

protein

But how does all that goodness get where it needs to go?

The answer is **digestion** — the way your food is broken down so your body can use it.

1. Food goes into your mouth, where it mixes with your **saliva** when you chew.

4. Your small intestine absorbs nutrients from the food and sends them into your body to do their work.

2. The food goes down a tube called the esophagus into your stomach.

5. Your large intestine absorbs water from the food and turns any unused food into waste.

3. The food is all mashed up into a kind of soup in your stomach.

6. The waste leaves your body when you go to the toilet.

21

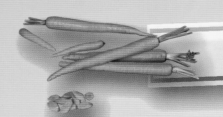

GLOSSARY

absorb: to soak up or take in something so it can be used.

balanced diet: meals and snacks that include the right foods, in the right amounts, from all of the food groups.

calcium: a silvery white, hard mineral that helps make bones and teeth strong.

carbohydrate: an important nutrient the body needs for energy. Carbohydrates are found in foods such as bread, pasta, and cereal, as well as in fruits and vegetables.

cells: the smallest parts of any living thing. The human body is made up of millions of cells.

dairy products: milk or cream and any foods made directly from milk or cream, such as cheese, ice cream, and yogurt.

digestion: the process of breaking down foods inside the body so their vitamins and other nutrients can be used.

digestive system: all the parts of the body that are used to digest food.

diseases: illnesses that make the body sick and keep it from working normally.

energy: the strength to perform physical or mental activity, or the heat or power needed for action or activity.

fat: a greasy or oily substance that helps the body absorb certain kinds of vitamins.

fiber: the part of a food that the body cannot break down and use through digestion. Fiber helps move food through the digestive system.

fluids: liquids.

infections: diseases or sores that are caused by germs and, often, can be passed on to other people.

iron: an important mineral that helps keep blood healthy. Iron is found in foods such as meats, spinach, dried beans, and apricots.

minerals: hard substances found in soil, water, and rocks, which are made up of things that have never been alive. The minerals in foods are important nutrients for the body.

nutrients: the nourishment in foods, including vitamins, minerals, fats, and protein, which the body needs to grow and to work properly.

protein: an important nutrient that helps the body make new cells and repair old ones. Protein is found in many kinds of foods, especially meats, beans, and dairy products.

saliva: a watery fluid that is made in the mouth and which starts the digestion of food.

servings: the amounts of foods you should eat at one time to take in enough of the nutrients the foods provide.

vitamins: thirteen nutrients the human body needs in small amounts to help turn food into energy and to stay healthy. The thirteen nutrients are vitamins A, C, D, E, K, and eight different types of B.

Here are some serving sizes for the main food groups.

carbohydrates: 1 slice of bread, 1/2 cup of cooked rice or pasta, 1 cup (a small bowl) of dry cereal

fruits and vegetables: 1 medium-size piece of fruit, 3/4 cup (a small glass) of fruit juice, 1/2 cup of chopped raw or cooked vegetables, 1 cup of leafy raw vegetables

protein: 1 medium-size hamburger, 2 fish sticks, 1 egg, 1/2 cup of baked beans, 2 tablespoons of peanut butter

dairy products: 1 cup of milk or yogurt, 2 cheese cubes (about the size of a pair of dice)

Could you answer all the questions? Here are the answers.

page 7: Spaghetti comes from Italy.

page 8: A tomato is a fruit.

page 11: Rhubarb is a vegetable.

page 12: People who do not eat meat or fish are called vegetarians.

page 15: We get milk from cows and, sometimes, from goats and sheep.

page 16: A doughnut has more fat.

page 19: A cucumber contains the most water.

INDEX